HENRY FORD

LYNN DAVIS

Consulting Editor, Diane Craig, M.A./Reading Specialist

Super Sandcastle

An Imprint of Abdo Publishing
abdopublishing.com

abdopublishing.com

Published by Abdo Publishing, a division of ABDO, PO Box 398166, Minneapolis, Minnesota 55439. Copyright © 2016 by Abdo Consulting Group, Inc. International copyrights reserved in all countries. No part of this book may be reproduced in any form without written permission from the publisher. Super SandCastle™ is a trademark and logo of Abdo Publishing.

Printed in the United States of America, North Mankato, Minnesota
062015
092015

THIS BOOK CONTAINS
RECYCLED MATERIALS

Editor: Liz Salzmann
Content Developer: Nancy Tuminelly
Cover and Interior Design and Production: Mighty Media, Inc.
Photo Credits: Library of Congress, Shutterstock, Wikicommons

Library of Congress Cataloging-in-Publication Data

Davis, Lynn, 1981- author.
Henry Ford / Lynn Davis ; consulting editor, Diane Craig, M.A./Reading Specialist.
     pages cm. -- (Amazing inventors & innovators)

Audience: K to grade 4
ISBN 978-1-62403-724-5

1. Ford, Henry, 1863-1947--Juvenile literature. 2. Automobile industry and trade--United States--Biography--Juvenile literature. 3. Industrialists--United States--Biography--Juvenile literature. 4. Automobile engineers--United States--Biography--Juvenile literature. I. Title.

TL140.F6D38 2016
338.7'6292'092--dc23
[B]
                    2014046600

Super SandCastle™ books are created by a team of professional educators, reading specialists, and content developers around five essential components—phonemic awareness, phonics, vocabulary, text comprehension, and fluency—to assist young readers as they develop reading skills and strategies and increase their general knowledge. All books are written, reviewed, and leveled for guided reading, early reading intervention, and Accelerated Reader™ programs for use in shared, guided, and independent reading and writing activities to support a balanced approach to literacy instruction.

CONTENTS

HENRY FORD

Ford with a Model T, 1921

Henry Ford was an American **innovator**. He didn't invent the car. But he made a better car. He knew how to make it at a low cost.

HENRY FORD

BORN: July 30, 1863, Greenfield Township, Michigan

MARRIAGE: Clara Ala Bryant, April 11, 1888

CHILDREN: Edsel Bryant

DIED: April 7, 1947, Dearborn, Michigan

MACHINE MASTER

Henry Ford was born on a farm. His father wanted him to be a farmer. But Henry was more interested in machines.

He became good at fixing watches. He learned about many other kinds of machines too.

Ford introduces a V-8 engine in 1932.

MAKING A BETTER CAR

Ford experimented with making a car. It had a gas engine.

Ford and his wife in the Quadricycle

Ford driving the Quadricycle

He called it the Ford Quadricycle. He made it in 1896.

RACING TOWARD VICTORY

Ford experimented with other kinds of cars. He even made a race car. It was called the "999" after the fastest train engine.

Barney Oldfield and Ford with the 999 race car, 1902

OTHER AUTO INNOVATORS

Karl Benz was German. He made the first modern car in 1885.

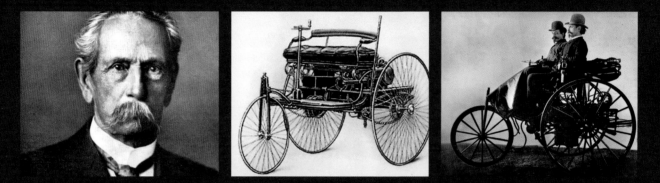

Ransom Eli Olds started the Oldsmobile company. It was in Lansing, Michigan. Oldsmobile began making cars in 1901. It used an **assembly line**.

RIDING A BESTSELLER

Ford made the Model N in 1907. It cost less than most other cars. It became the best-selling car in the country.

Ford in a Model N outside the Ford Piquette Plant, Detroit, Michigan

Ford Model N Runabouts

THE MODEL T

Henry Ford was not satisfied. He wanted to make a better car at an even lower price. He made the Model T in 1908.

It cost less than the Model N. More people could buy one.

MODEL T PARTS

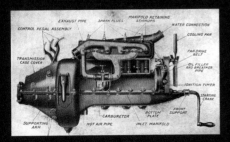

Model T engine

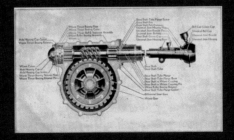

Model T truck axle

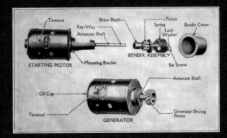

Model T starter and generator units

A NEW FACTORY

The Model T was very popular. People bought as many as the company could make.

Ford Model T assembly line, about 1914

Henry Ford wanted to make a lot more Model Ts.
The company moved to a new factory in 1910.
It was in Highland Park, Michigan.

BIGGER, BETTER, FASTER, STRONGER

The new factory was much bigger. The car parts were **standardized**.

Highland Park assembly line, 1913

The **assembly line** moved. The factory workers could produce many more cars.

Highland Park assembly line, 1913

BACK IN BLACK

At first the Model T came in different colors. But then Ford sped up the assembly line. Black paint dried fastest. So all Model Ts were painted black.

POWER TO THE PEOPLE

The Model T was a big success. It was easy to make. It had a low price.

Highland Park assembly line, 1924

Ford's friend Thomas Edison with a Ford Motel T, 1928

Henry Ford made it possible for the average person to own a car!

MORE ABOUT FORD

Ford knew **THOMAS EDISON**. Edison **encouraged** Ford's work with cars.

Ford once ran for a seat in the **US SENATE**. He didn't win.

Ford died in 1947. All **traffic** in Detroit stopped for **ONE MINUTE** to honor him.

TEST YOUR KNOWLEDGE

1. What was Henry Ford good at fixing?

2. What was the name of Henry Ford's first car?

3. All Model Ts were painted blue. True or false?

THINK ABOUT IT!

What kind of car would you build?

ANSWERS: 1. Watches 2. Ford Quadricycle 3. False

23

GLOSSARY

assembly line – a way of making something in which the item moves from worker to worker until it is finished.

encourage – to urge or try to convince.

innovator – someone who does something in a new way.

standardize – to make or do the same way each time.

traffic – the cars and trucks driving on streets and highways.